CW00733687

The Role of a
Christian Mother

by
Anna Melchior

*All booklets are published thanks to the
generous support of the members of the
Catholic Truth Society*

CATHOLIC TRUTH SOCIETY
PUBLISHERS TO THE HOLY SEE

Contents

Introduction

Congratulations! You are a mother or about to become one. As a mother, you are or will be doing the most fundamental job there is: raising children. The work of a mother is extremely important, difficult and tiring, and profoundly rewarding. This little book aims to support you in your work as a mother.

Even experienced mothers want additional support from time to time because being a mother is quite like being a Christian in that we are always apprentices, never masters, of our vocation. It is helpful, therefore, frequently to remind ourselves of the principles of what we do - the profound motivation, the basic strategies, the long-term aims - principles that are easily lost sight of in the daily struggle to get this here thing done now.

In the following pages, I consider the enormous significance and challenges of mothering, suggest ground rules of action and interaction that can make mothering easier, and point out the many-layered relevance of the Christian faith to the work of a mother. I hope that reading this booklet will help you to experience the incredible joy that is the reward of being a mother.

Responsibilities

The responsibilities of mothers are awesome. By loving your children, you enable your children to love themselves and to love others. By respecting your children and meeting their needs, you show your children that the world is a safe place to be. By providing a good example, discussing your goals and hopes with your children, and setting boundaries, you give your children values that will support and guide them throughout their lives. By encouraging your children to contribute to the on-going team effort that is the family, you teach your children to act responsibly. By sharing your faith with your children you help your children to believe and trust in God and to put their faith into practice. By loving your children, meeting their needs, sharing your values with them, giving them responsibilities they can handle, and teaching them about your faith, you help them to become well-adjusted, responsible adults capable of loving others and of a deep, sustaining faith. The effective communication of love, security, values, a sense of responsibility, and of faith depends on a bond based on unconditional love. This is why an institutional childcare setting, no matter how well run, cannot communicate these fundamentals to children anywhere near as effectively as mothers can. The work of mothers, therefore, is necessary to the functioning of our homes, our communities, our society, our economy, and to the future of the Church.

Challenges

The challenges mothers confront are also awesome. A friend of ours expressed this succinctly: "They said it would be hard, but it was harder".[1] As a mother, you give of yourself for up to twenty-four hours a day; you are permanently on call. You have to acquire diverse knowledge and apply it to the task at hand; being a mother can require you to learn about allergies one day, guinea pigs the next, and school policy on the third. You make small as well as big decisions almost constantly and generally quickly and independently and have to keep in mind the, at times, big implications of small decisions. You manage people in all their complexity, diverse situations, ever-changing logistical requirements, a budget, and a household: mothering is the management challenge par excellence because it requires the simultaneous management of disparate areas. As a mother, moreover, you need to remain flexible and persevere because being a mother is the one job from which you cannot walk away. There are no other jobs quite as challenging as being a mother because mothering challenges you on all levels - physically, emotionally, intellectually, and spiritually. At the same time, mothering is generally looked down upon in our society and considered a worthless occupation, easily

---

[1] A mother of three by adoption.

replaced by professional childcare, ready meals, and computer games. And it is unpaid. Those who nonetheless opt to mother tend to find themselves isolated from the rest of society, outcasts from the prestige-seeking, money-driven mainstream. This makes being a mother even more challenging.

God is your support and guide

It is just as well then that, as a Christian, you know that God is at your side. The Christian faith is a fantastic resource for mothers. Your faith helps you to recognise the importance of what you are doing. We venerate Mary, the mother of God, not because she was heroic, learned, wealthy, or powerful. We venerate her because she was a mother and, through her mothering, taught us about the demands and the blessings of a life lived for others. Your faith, moreover, is an excellent guide to mothering. You cannot do better than to consider how God loves and guides you and try to emulate His example in loving and guiding your own children. Good mothering is as simple, and as difficult, as that. Your faith, finally, offers support in times of trial. Faith deepens your love, focuses your vision, enriches your understanding, and teaches you to submit to the will of God which you know to be good. And it is from such rich soil that hope can grow. And hope is the driving force of mothering.

When you delve the depths of your faith as you confront the responsibilities and challenges of being a mother, you will find there sustenance, guidance, and hope. Your relationship to God helps you to love, to forgive, to persevere, and to hope. When you can love, forgive, persevere, and hope, you can build enduring relationships with others; you can share yourself with others, do your duty, and cope with difficulties. You can fulfil the responsibilities and meet the challenges of being a mother. When you think of your work as a mother as faith in action, your work is enriched by your faith and enriches your faith. Mothering helps you to grow as a Christian.

Loving your child

The love that underpins your attitudes and actions towards your children is what, more than anything else, makes you a mother. It is central to your identity as a mother and central to your relationship with your children. It is also the foundation of all that you will ever be able to teach your children. But feeling love for your baby in the early days when you are overwhelmed and exhausted and the two of you may be effectively strangers can be difficult. And expressing your love to your growing children when time pressures, diverging values, and your children's occasionally unfathomable behaviour pull you apart, can also prove challenging. Before considering these issues, let us look at God's love for you to help us understand better the source and nature of a mother's love.

God's love for you

God loves you like the perfect mother. He loves you unconditionally. He loves you when you succeed and when you struggle; He loves you when you are kind and when you are angry; He loves you when you rejoice and when you suffer. God's love is, moreover, transformative.

It is 'an effective and operative love. [it] is a love which, far from presupposing in us any lovableness, actually produces that lovableness within us.'[2] God's love lifts you up, as it were, out of your own ways and into His way; it helps you to grow in virtue. God's love, then, is unconditional and it is enabling. God loves you even when you fail to be kind and wise and good. And God's love enables you to become kind and wise and good.

Practising your faith can help you to experience God's love. When you keep in mind God' s word as you go about your activities, when you devote time to prayer, read spiritual texts, attend Mass, seek out the sacrament of reconciliation, and give as well as receive love through countless acts of kindness, you can come to know and enjoy God's love for you. You can come to feel yourself held by Him and guided by Him and experience the joy of being known and loved. And when you know yourself to be loved by Him as His child with an unconditional and enabling love, you can come to love yourself with an unconditional and enabling love. When you know yourself to be loved by Him as His child with an unconditional and enabling love, you can also come to love your children with an unconditional and enabling love.

---

[2] Garrigou-Lagrange, O.P., G. (1977) *The Three Ways of the Interior Life*, Tan Books, Rockford, Illinois, p 9.

Margaret Hebblethwaite, a Catholic mother and author, captures the link between God's love for us and our love for our children:

> When we fail we need to turn to the one who has not failed, in whom hope and achievement are perfectly united, in whom motherly love has lived up to its promise.[...] We have already drunk deeply, more deeply than we know, of that divine love, and have our children drink of it through us. But it is not ours to give for ever, it does not originate in us. We must turn back, and drink again, like children, trust again, pray again, depend again. Then, strengthened and consoled by our mother, we can be a mother again to our little ones, letting maternity flow through us, not from us but from God.[3]

Like God's love for you, your unconditional love for your children enables your children to grow in holiness and happiness. Your unconditional love for your children communicates acceptance, respect, and concern to your children. This helps your children to experience their life as worthwhile and to develop self-confidence and trust in others. From this position of profound security, your children are enabled to engage with the world and to

---

[3] Hebblethwaite, Margaret (1984) *Motherhood and God*, Geoffrey Chapman, London, p70.

develop loving relationships - to pass on, in effect, the love they have received.

As you let God's love flow through you to hold and to guide your children, you yourself become changed. When you love your children unconditionally, you give of yourself without looking to your own advantage. And as you give of yourself to your children, you find that your children become a part of you. You are then at once diminished in finite external assets such as money and professional prestige as you pour of yourself - your time, your energy, your dreams, your ambitions - into these little beings, and infinitely enriched internally by these new lives and this new love.

Becoming a mother

Motherhood comes as a shock to many women. As most women in the Western world have little to no experience of babies before having their own, they are unprepared for the challenges of young motherhood. Sleepless, exhausted, confined to the house, and isolated from friends and colleagues, they may wonder what they have brought upon themselves and feel not a little resentful towards their baby whose demanding presence is upsetting their world and, with their world, their sense of self. In addition, mothering a baby involves rapidly learning many new skills, such as bathing and breastfeeding the baby, as well as acquiring a vast amount of new knowledge, such as that pertaining to a baby's dietary requirements and signs of illness in a baby. Learning these skills and acquiring this knowledge can be a nerve-wrecking, anxiety-ridden process as your baby's well-being hinges on your success. Most babies are very demanding, moreover, and all babies are entirely dependent. Mothering a baby therefore also involves, initially, at any rate, focusing entirely on the needs of your child. If you were used to having some time to yourself as well as time to engage in paid employment, this may be difficult. Mothering, finally, is a low status occupation in our society as it is unpaid and - wrongly - considered not to require much in the way of skills and knowledge. If you enjoyed professional status, then becoming a mother can seriously shake your identity. Here is how one mother described this experience:

> There was a way in which having that first baby shook everything for me - the bits of me that weren't central started flying off in all directions, and then you're left with this question of what is there left in the middle and what am I really about.[4]

Note that this mother said that it was the bits not central to her identity that became lost to her when she became a mother. This point is important. The cliché

---

[4] Cited in Figes, Kate (1998) *Life after Birth*, Penguin Books, London, p 39.

about losing your identity when you become a mother is, it seems to me, a tired one and a false one. Far from losing your identity when you become a mother, becoming a mother is a chance to find out who you are when you are stripped of the trappings on which your identity superficially hinged. Once you are over the initial shock and exhaustion of new motherhood, there is a good chance that you will find plenty of opportunity to be yourself in and through your work as a mother. A mother I know with a love of photography takes photos of her two small children; another is an illustrator and has taught one of her children to draw and visits galleries with both her teenage children; an extremely funny mother has got a very funny child; I take our children on walking holidays and discuss environmental issues, theology, and washing-up methods with the older two. With a little imagination, you can integrate your whole personality as well as your interests into your mothering. A formerly high-powered PR executive discovered that being a mother allowed her 'to unite all my life's experience in what I'm doing right now... I can't imagine another job where I can do that.'[5] Becoming a mother is, moreover, a chance to add depth and dimension to your identity as you slowly but surely become someone who is defined first and foremost by their love. Becoming a mother is a journey of self-discovery which is frightening indeed, but also tremendously rewarding. The bestselling author Erica Jong writes about motherhood:

> Its demands are so compelling, so clearly important, and also so profoundly satisfying. ...You give up yourself, and finally you don't even mind. You become your child's guide to life at the expense of that swollen ego you thought so immutable. I wouldn't have missed this for anything. It humbled my ego and stretched my soul. It awakened me to eternity. It made me know my own humanity, my own mortality, my own limits. It gave me whatever crumbs of wisdom I possess today.[6]

Having that first baby is a major life change. It helps to decide deliberately to take this time apart and to live it in the moment, without plans and preconceptions crowding between you and your baby. The period after the birth is a period of transition for you; your body as well as your heart, mind, and spirit are undergoing a process of reconfiguration.[7] Your sense of self changes as you gradually become a mother to your baby. Let your baby be your guide in this process. As you are available, attentive, and responsive to your baby, you find that you gradually

---

[6] Erica Jong in *Fear of Fifty*, quoted in Exley, Helen (1998), *Thoughts on Being a Mother*, Exley Publications, New York.

[7] A good book to guide you through this period is Stern, Daniel N. (1998), *The Birth of a Mother*, Bloomsbury, London.

ease into your new identity as a mother while also laying the foundation of your relationship with your child and your child's life.[8] This time in your life cannot be subjected to the usual pressures of the outside world, pressures that demand routine, control, efficiency, immaculate appearance, measurable achievement, and recognisable success. Breastfeeding is a particularly striking illustration of this point. Breastfeeding can be difficult, awkward, and utterly unglamorous and its success, measured in amounts drunk, impossible to ascertain. And yet - given time - breastfeeding can become a wonderful and hugely beneficial experience for both you and your child.[9] The standards of the world of work are irrelevant to the mother-baby relationship which is about intimacy, getting to know each other, and, above all, about love.

Get as much help as you can to start with so that you have guidance in looking after your baby as well as people around to look after you. You may want to draw up a rota for your friends and relatives prior to the birth of your baby and get them to commit to bringing meals round, doing some shopping and cleaning, and simply sitting with you and holding the baby during the first few weeks after the birth. Ideally, your husband or a close friend or relative can take time off work and be there for you and the baby in the days

---

[8] Adopting a child of any age requires a process of adjustment similar to the one described in this paragraph.

[9] For help with breastfeeding, see *laleche.org.uk*.

after the birth. It would also be helpful if you could get in touch with one or two experienced mothers while you are still pregnant who could then give you advice as well as assistance after the birth of your first-born. Such a system of mothers' mentors, if it became as common as ante-natal classes and were funded by the government, could contribute significantly to the well-being of mothers, babies, and families by helping to give them a good start.

Given time and support, you will learn the skills and acquire the knowledge needed to mother your baby. Given time and support, you will also come to love your baby. As you get to know your baby, looking after your baby becomes easier because you are able to interpret more accurately your baby's cries and expressions and to respond more effectively. And as looking after your baby becomes easier, you come to enjoy your baby more. And as you come to enjoy your baby more, you fall in love with your baby. As your love for your baby grows, so does your enjoyment of your baby. This is how one mother recalls falling in love with her baby:

> I had discovered true love. The love which repays slavery and exhaustion with a brief smile. But what a smile! It was more than enough. My present prostration was somehow sweeter than all the pleasure of my past life.[10]

---

[10] Sue Limb in *Love Forty*, quoted in Exley, Helen (1998), *Thoughts on Being a Mother*, Exley Publications, New York.

By doing what is best for your baby, then, you are helping yourself to enjoy being a mother. By meeting the demands of love, you come to enjoy the rewards of love. In my book *Mothering*, I refer to this as 'the lovely loop'[11] - and lovely it is indeed when what is virtuous is also pleasurable!

Expressing your love for your child

Once you have fallen in love with your baby, expressing your love for your baby will probably come easily. You want to hold your baby and cuddle your baby, snuggle up to your baby, look at your baby, listen to your baby, talk and sing to your baby, and play with your baby. All these activities communicate your love to your baby provided they are geared to your baby's personality and needs. A disregard for your baby's personality and needs in your interaction with your baby, for example through overstimulation, would confuse and irritate your baby. It is absolutely vital, therefore, that you take the time to get to know your baby. By taking that time you can help your baby to grow up healthy and happy as babies who enjoy plenty of loving, sympathetic contact with their mothers develop better physically, emotionally, and mentally[12].

---

[11] Melchior, Anna (2007) *Mothering - a spiritual and practical approach*, St Pauls, London, p81.

[12] The more babies are spoken to - by a person, not by a tape or the radio - for instance, the more intelligent they will become, according to research cited in *The Herald Tribune*, 18th April 1997.

Letting your baby sleep in your bed with you and carrying your baby on your back can help your baby to feel loved and secure and to gain weight more quickly. Sharing your bed with your baby is safe for your baby unless you or your husband are drunk, drugged, smokers, or excessively tired. Do make sure, of course, that your baby's head is not covered by a blanket or duvet. When you need to go out or do jobs around the house, putting your baby into a sling enables you to keep your baby close by - smelling your familiar smell and feeling your familiar movements - while you get on with other things. I found that both practices make mothering a baby a great deal easier: keeping our babies in our bed at night ensured that I got the sleep I needed and carrying our babies on my back from about three months[13] enabled me to engage with the rest of the world - by cuddling an older child, cooking, writing, shopping, travelling, even teaching - while looking after our babies.

Do share your baby with your husband, older children, parents and parents-in-law and close friends! Sharing your baby with others who also love your baby can give you precious time to recharge either by resting or by doing what you enjoy doing without your baby. Provided you are your baby's main carer, the additional stimulation provided by other carers is beneficial and enjoyable for

---

[13] in the *Wilkinet Baby Carrier.*

your baby. It is, moreover, wise to give other family members and close friends the time and opportunity to develop their own relationships with your baby because, by and by, you want your child to become part of a network of loving relationships that will help to strengthen and guide your child and provide a sympathetic, child-friendly community for you both.

As your children grow up, love continues to require time to grow as well as time to show. After the shock of early motherhood has subsided, spending time with your children remains the essence of the lovely loop, the virtuous spiral in which you continually get to know your children, fall in love with your children, express your love for your children and discover that, as you express your love for your children, your love for them increases. Spending time with your children allows you to stay in touch with who your children are and are becoming and to respond to your children's needs and concerns as they arise. Spending time with your children also feeds them with the knowledge of being loved and of being part of a family that has particular values and traditions, interests and tastes. Spending time with your children gives your children a sense of belonging, which is the basis of healthy growth.

An aside of a political nature is in order here. Rather than pressurising mothers back to full-time work as soon as possible after giving birth and putting the burden for children's development on schools (which can only do too little, too late), governments could choose to afford mothers - and fathers! - more time with their children by giving them extended and flexible parental leave, tax breaks, part-time jobs, and flexible working hours as well as advice and support. Contrary to the impression given by current political propaganda, incidentally, most mothers *want* to be able to spend more time with their children.[14] With their mothers and fathers spending more time with them at home, children would have a chance to become grounded in their family culture and to feel loved and appreciated. Without that chance, children can easily grow up disoriented, a ready target for existential angst and its many pseudo cures such as drugs, alcohol, and casual sex.

Small children enjoy having their mother available, perhaps for half an hour to an hour a day to join in their games. I used to sit on the floor in the children's room for a while most afternoons when our older two were little. I would cut up and distribute apples and oranges, and wait for our children to engage me, or not, in their imaginative

---

[14] According to figures cited in a UK government document entitled *Choice for Parents: The Best Start for Children*, published by the Treasury in December 2004, 63% of British mothers in employment would like to work fewer hours and nearly half of all working mothers (44%) would prefer to give up work altogether to stay at home with their children if they could afford to do so. See also the book by the sociologist Catherine Hakim (2000) *Work-Lifestyle Choices in 21st Century: Preference Theory*, Oxford University Press, Oxford.

play. This gave me a chance to observe their fascinating imagination at work and, because I was there for them - available, attentive, and responsive - it showed our children that I loved them. Now that we have four children and they and I are increasingly busy, our evening meals ensure that we all come together at least once a day. Eating together - at a table, without a television or radio running - is a good way of developing family life. It provides the opportunity to keep in touch with each other through conversation, to learn to be considerate by listening and observing decent table manners, and to enjoy home-cooked food. At present, only fifty per cent of UK families eat together three or more times a week.[15] That's sad.

For school children of all ages, a welcoming kitchen is likely to be a great attraction. There they can sit and rest and draw or do homework, get a drink and a snack, be near their mother and assist her as she prepares the evening meal or washes up, and perhaps, ever so casually, tell her about the day's events and ask her for help or advice. Doing jobs together with your children is generally an effective way of spending time together with your children while showing them that you appreciate them and their efforts. Walking places with your children is also a pleasant way of being together. Reading to your children at bedtime is another mutually beneficial way of

---

[15] See *rasingkids.co.uk* for more information.

sharing time as well as an interest which need not be reserved only for small children.

The most important way of expressing your love to your children of any age is to listen to them. When you listen to your children, you show them that you are interested in them and in what they have to say and that you care for them and their well-being. This knowledge gives your children a profound sense of security and self-confidence which, in turn, enables them to relate to others. When listening to your children, it is helpful to maintain eye contact at the same level and occasionally to reflect back your children's statements so that they know you are listening. Avoid jumping in with your own judgments and reactions. Instead, show your children that you accept them and their thoughts and feelings. This allows your children to reach their own conclusions and find their own solutions, though they may need your help in thinking constructively about a situation.

Praying together as a family in the evenings, finally, gives you all a chance to share with each other your gratitude, regrets, hopes, and worries as you reflect together on the day and anticipate the next. Praying together allows you and your children to remind yourselves of the good in your lives, such as the fine weather and others' kind deeds, and to give thanks to God. Praying together allows you and your children to acknowledge wrong-doing, such as hitting and intentionally annoying others, and become reconciled again to God and to each other. And praying together allows you and your children to express your concerns, about school or a relative's health, perhaps, and to entrust them to His loving will. Held, then, by Him, you are better equipped to hold each other lovingly through the daily trials and triumphs of family life.

Guiding your child

When you love your child, you want what is best for your child. And as you know that what is best for your child does not simply come about without any effort on you and your child's part, you try and guide your child towards what is good. Guiding your child is mainly a matter of communicating your values to your child by providing good example and setting boundaries. Love is not only the motive but also the mainstay of this process of guiding your child. 'Only if our children know that we love them, will they be inclined to pay attention to, ponder, and respond positively to our attempts to guide them.'[16] When you are motivated by love and express your love to your child and are ready as well as able to let love overcome resentment or disappointment and to forgive, then your efforts to guide your child will bear fruit.

Providing a good example

What you do and how you do it and what you talk about and how you talk about it reflect your attitudes to your children, to other people, and to the wider world. Based

---

[16] Melchior, Anna (2007) *Mothering - a spiritual and practical approach*, St Pauls, London, p 109.

in large part on the attitudes communicated through your actions and words, your children devise their own value systems. Those value systems or moral frameworks inform your children's understanding of themselves and of society and therefore their behaviour. So, what you do and say matters, a lot.

At a practical level, you can teach your children about consideration for others and about the value of food and much else besides simply by engaging them in your activities around the house. As your children pick up the skills it takes to run a household, they also pick up the values expressed in your daily round of chores. Just think of everything your work in the home says about you! When you put away your shoes and coat, it tells your children that you value tidiness. When you clean the bathroom, it tells your children that you value cleanliness. When you spend time cooking, it tells your children that you value fresh food. When you keep left-overs and make sure that all the food you buy is consumed rather than binned, it tells your children that you avoid waste.[17] When you adhere to the LOAF principles when shopping for food and buy food that is locally produced, organically grown, animal friendly, and fairly traded,[18] your children

---

[17] In the UK, one third of all food bought ends up in the bin. See *lovefoodhatewaste.com* for ideas and advice on how to stop this waste.

[18] See the Christian Ecology Link, *christian-ecology.org.uk*; and have a look at CAFOD's *livesimply* challenge.

learn to value the local economy, the environment, animal welfare, and the quality of the lives of the people producing your food. When you avoid packaging whenever possible, recycle rubbish, switch off lights that are not needed, use water sparingly, and walk and cycle (etc, etc, etc), your children, too, will end up with good habits that will help them as well as others. And if you give your children a chance to join in the work as well as in the decision-making processes involved in the work and get your husband in on the act, as well, these habits will help to shape your children's values.

In addition to your work around the house, your children also observe how you run your own life. Do you take time to exercise? Do you meet up with friends and relations? Are you hospitable? Generous? Do you take an interest in community events, in politics, sports, the theatre, music, art? Do you attend Mass at least once a week? Do you gladly do favours for others? Are you generally punctual? What books do you read? What television programmes do you watch? On what do you spend your money? How do you cope with illness? Everything you do expresses your values. And your children, clever and observant as children are, learn from your example not only what to do but also what to think and even what to feel. Research indicates that our own example above all else determines whether or not our children will have a well developed faith, for instance.[19] God willing, we will not have to follow in the footsteps of St Margaret Clitherow, wife, mother, convert and martyr who set up a school for Catholic children, harboured priests in her home, and was executed in the reign of Elizabeth I, but our own devotion to the sacraments, commitment to the teachings of the Church, and little daily sacrifices can still teach our children most powerfully that our faith is profoundly worthwhile.

You communicate your values to your children not only through what you do but also through what you say and don't say. What stories do you tell your children? What questions do you ask them? Do you listen to them? How do you respond to their questions? Do you swear? Do you gossip? Do you complain a lot? Do you pass judgment? Do you discuss important decisions as a family? Do you say grace before meals? Do you talk with your children about God? You teach your children about respecting others, for example, primarily by respecting them. If you take the time to listen to your children, your children learn about the art of listening to others and they learn about respecting the thoughts and feelings of others. And this will help to make your children not only more secure and kinder individuals but also individuals genuinely capable of learning from others.

---

[19] cf Strommel, Merton and Hardel, Richard (2002) *Passing on the Faith*, Saint Mary's Press.

A great advantage of teaching your children by providing good example is that your children can pick up as much or as little from your actions and words as they are prepared to understand. Children develop at different rates in different respects and have different personalities. While one child may want to join in an activity you are engaged in - say, repairing your bicycle - and learn all about it, for instance, another will barely notice what you are doing. Similarly, one child may tune in to a conversation her parents are having about a cousin's baptism, for example, and ask questions about it, while another continues to focus on her game as the conversation is carried on in the background. As long as you provide your children with plenty of opportunities to join in, listen in, and ask questions, and leave it up to your children to respond to these opportunities, you will teach your children about the world and their place in it through real, hands-on experience at a pace that matches and appropriately stretches their abilities and interests.

Guiding your children by providing good example obviously requires that you spend time with your children. A few words about the distinction between so-called quality and quantity time, or, as Frank Furedi, author of *Paranoid Parenting* puts it, between 'engaged' and 'accessible' time are necessary here. While time spent engaging directly with your children is certainly very important, we underestimate the importance of merely accessible time spent with our children at their peril. A child's upbringing is to a large extent shaped by time spent with a parent who is present and available but not focusing on the child. It is only when children are integrated to some extent in the life of adults that they can learn from those adults and about such life and that you can effectively pass on your values to your children. Children learn a great deal by observing their parents at work in the house, interacting with each other as well as with other adults, and pursuing their own interests. By spending time with your children as you cook, read a book, discuss a job with the builder, talk with your friends, listen to music, mend a shirt, dig in the vegetable plot, prepare for a feast day, and so forth, you allow your children to learn about the world, the work, the manners, and the values of adults. Your children also learn that they cannot always expect to be the focus of their parents' attention whenever their parents are around. These lessons prepare them in many ways better for adult life than regular thirty-minute sessions of quality time.

With children increasingly farmed out to all-day nurseries and breakfast and after-school clubs as well as holiday schemes, they have less chance to learn from their parents' example. Nursery and school teachers cannot replace parents in providing good example because children do not witness their teachers in a great variety of situations and engaged in a great variety of activities - the institutional environment of a nursery or school necessarily limits what a teacher can teach children. In addition, the bond of unconditional love is missing in the teacher-child relationship which renders any lessons taught necessarily less effective.[20]

Setting boundaries

In an ideal world, perhaps, all you would need to do would be to provide good example and your children would follow suit and become as kind and generous, as conscientious and diligent, as devout and wise as you are. But this is not an ideal world. I, for one, am not as kind and generous, as conscientious and diligent, and as devout and wise as I would like to be and would like our children to be. So I am definitely a defective good example to our children. Society around us, moreover, does not consistently promote and reward kindness and generosity, conscientiousness and diligence, devoutness and wisdom. As a result, our children are generally presented with defective good examples at school, on television, with their friends. In a less than ideal world, therefore, we need to do more than to provide good example to guide our children. We need to give our

---

[20] The UK government wants to hold schools accountable for the behaviour of pupils, including drug problems, obesity, criminal behaviour, and teenage pregnancies - a plan teachers' unions have condemned as 'ridiculous', *The Times*, 6th May 2008.

children boundaries, we need to give them rules and reasons to help guide their behaviour.

The purpose of rules is three-fold. Rules help children to *discover the world*. By insisting that your children try this and do that - and keep trying this and doing that even when it does not immediately appeal - you help your children to broaden their experience as well as to discover the rewards of perseverance. I struggled for several years, for instance, to get our eldest daughter to practise the piano and the violin. She clearly had talent and I did not want to see that talent go to waste. I also wanted her to discover for herself that greater skill leads to greater enjoyment. Our now fifteen-year old daughter greatly enjoys playing her instruments these days and actually said to me the other week, 'thanks, mum, for making me practise.' I was, you will appreciate, thrilled to bits.

Rules also help children to *engage with others*. If they have learned considerate ways of interaction, if they know to look out for and to respond to other people's needs and to respect other people's points of view, if they know how to make their own needs and points of view known without offending, chances are they will be able to manage even challenging encounters comfortably and competently. Especially when you have several children, harmonious family life depends on your children observing rules of behaviour that facilitate sharing, co-operating, and dealing constructively with conflict.[21] Having and getting on with siblings teaches children a lot about themselves, about others, and about relationships, and is fantastic preparation for adult life.

Rules, finally, help children to *make sense* of the bewildering bombardment of impressions to which we are all subjected; they provide children with a compass to steer through and past sundry influences. Rules help your children to sort and sieve information, to differentiate the frivolous from the worthwhile and the beneficial from the harmful, and to guide them to seek deeper understanding. By giving your children rules and discussing with them your reasons for those rules, you help your children to think about the flow of data directed at them. A very modern temptation, for example, is to consider ourselves knowledgeable about and in control of something because we have access to information on it. Sex is a case in point. Older children are inundated with information about sex from schools and the media which fools them into specious confidence that they understand sex and can deal with its physical and psychological consequences. Information, however, is not the same as understanding. With your help, your children will realise that information alone does not in fact equip them to understand and cope with sex. Only a framework of

---

[21] For help with this, see Faber, Adele and Mazlish, Elaine (1998), *Siblings without Rivalry*, Piccadilly, London.

values, such as the dignity of the person, along with the maturity that comes with learning to submit whims to higher goals can render your children capable of dealing with this particular complex phenomenon, and many others besides.

To set boundaries for your children effectively, you need values and time. You cannot set boundaries for your children, you cannot give your children rules and explain to them the reasons for those rules, if you lack values to determine both rules and reasons. In other words, in order to pass on a moral framework to your children, you need to have one yourself. And the more aware you are of your own moral framework, the more you have thought about it and deliberately tried to live in accordance with it, the more convincing a teacher to your children you will be. Your faith is a great asset here, for faith guides your reason towards meanings and values and hence towards a moral framework. Faith also helps you to distinguish between what really matters and what is less important so you are sure to fight battles that are worth the effort; consideration for others, for example, would command higher priority than tidiness. Faith, moreover, provides you with the motivation to follow rules because we know that God only wants what is best for us. Faith is both the guiding light and the bedrock of any moral framework and you cannot do better than to pass on your faith to your children.

In addition to a moral framework, you need time with your children. Spending time with your children helps you to know where your children are at, which rules they need now, and what reasons they are capable of understanding. Knowing your children well is very important for the effective transmission of a values system - and another reason why teachers cannot easily transmit values to a class of thirty-odd pupils. In order to communicate rules to your children, you also need to make your expectations clear to them and that, too, takes time together. In addition, you need to be able to trust your children, and trust, as well, is only developed over time spent together. To give your children boundaries, therefore, you need to spend time with your children in which you share responsibility with your children, depend on your children, praise them for their efforts, explain to your children your own actions, and listen to and take on board their perspectives - time, in other words, in which you work, play, and talk with your children. As you spend time with your children, you come to know what they are capable of and to trust them to act responsibly when you are not with them. Setting boundaries for your children helps your children to negotiate society and it helps you to let go of your children.[22]

---

[22] For further advice on how to set boundaries as well as general advice and support with parenting in a variety of formats - from publications and tapes to courses, workshops, and lectures - see *familycaringtrust.co.uk* and the website of the Family Life Ministry, *flm.org.uk*.

The current tendency to overprotect children and hem them in with a continuous schedule of organised activity is, I am convinced, due in part to an increasing lack of trust of parents in their children. This lack of trust, in turn, is largely due to the children's exclusion from their parents' lives. By spending time with your children, you can communicate rules to them and develop trust in your children's ability to understand and to follow those rules. And once you have developed that trust, you can give your children the freedom they need to learn to manage themselves.

Forgiving

Guiding your children, then, involves providing good example and engaging them in it, making your expectations clear, giving reasons for your rules, and learning to trust your children to live up to your expectations. None of this achieves anything, however, without plenty of forgiving thrown in, as well. Not one of us is perfect and all of us fail to live up to our own and others' expectations at one point or another. The practice of forgiving is therefore an essential element of the process of transmitting values to children.

I often fall short of my own expectations. I am, for example, apt to lose my temper when I feel hassled by too many demands made on me, and that is not a good thing. So, over the years, I have learned to apologise. And that is a very good thing. When you apologise to your children, your children learn that the rules you teach them, such as those pertaining to respect and consideration for others, also apply to you - that you do not stand above the rules. By witnessing your struggle to live according to your values, moreover, your children come to appreciate the importance of those values and the effort required to live up to them. They also come to appreciate the need for humility in any learning process.

By acknowledging your errors and asking your children to forgive you, moreover, you give your children the chance to learn to forgive. You help them to draw the fundamental Christian distinction between the sin and the sinner. You help them to realise that they do not have to approve everything somebody does because they love them, or else reject a person because they reject what they have done. You teach them that they can reject what somebody has done without rejecting them, that they can continue to love where they cannot approve. You teach them that they can offer others a second chance, an opportunity to leave past errors behind and to move on. You also teach them that they can help themselves to overcome hurt, anger, and resentment by forgiving others. The capacity to forgive, more than anything else, will equip your children for adult relationships.

Your children also need to know that you will not judge them by their actions. Whether they have spilled their juice, done badly in an exam, or lashed out at their brother in anger, your children need to know that your love for them is always hopeful, persevering, and forgiving. They need to know that, while you have high expectations of them because you love them and want what is best for them, you will still love them and want what is best for them when they fail to live up to those expectations. They need to know that you can dissociate them from their actions and that you can keep your love and hope for them alive even when you have been disappointed or hurt by their actions. Your children need to know, moreover, that you want to help them to learn from failure. Your children need to know that you are always ready to embrace them and always ready to help them to get up and try again.

By readily forgiving your children, you also keep intact your positive attitude towards your children, and your positive attitude towards your children is your children's greatest motivator. When your children sense from your words and actions that you think of them as kind and responsible human beings, they are much more likely to become kind and responsible human beings! Specific positive feedback[23] is much more effective than criticism or punishment. So forgive your children readily, do not harbour resentment, and encourage your children in all the good that they do.

---

[23] Being specific is important, so 'it was very kind of you to share your cake with Tom', for example, is more effective than 'you were a good girl today'.

In your efforts to guide your children, the Church is there to guide you by providing good example in the life of Christ and the lives of saints, with sound teaching on moral issues, and through the sacrament of reconciliation which helps you and your older children to return to God's embrace and guiding hand whenever you have failed. God's love for you, just as your love for your children, is forever hopeful, persevering, and forgiving. His love shows you the path of righteousness and helps you back onto it when you have strayed. Do then, take advantage of this great source of light and strength as you help your children to discover, engage with, and understand the world.

Persevering through difficulties

As much as I would like to think of being a mother as an unending round of joyful activities interspersed with moments of pure bliss, I know I would be fooling myself, and you. Being a mother is a great source of joy, yes, but it is also a great source of strain, stress, and anxiety. Acknowledging our need for help may present a hurdle at first as we would probably all like to think of ourselves as perfectly capable and competent to deal with whatever our role as mother throws at us. But few, if any, mothers never fail to manage. Once you have acknowledged your need for help and identified specifically in which areas you would benefit from help, however, there is much you can do to help yourself.

Easing your workload

Energy is, perhaps, the *sine qua non* of mothering - if you haven't got any, you cannot respond to the needs of your children and to the demands of the household. However, if you are constantly responding to the needs of your children and to the demands of the household, you don't have energy left for other pursuits. One solution to this dilemma is to invest some energy into *reducing* both the needs of your children and the demands of the household.

One strategy for easing your workload is to combine looking after your children with doing household chores. When you combine housework with looking after your children, you do not spend your slots of childfree time doing household chores. And that is good for you. When you combine housework with looking after your children, moreover, your children learn to occupy themselves, without your input. And when your children have the ability to occupy themselves, life is more enjoyable for them and a lot easier for you. When you combine housework with looking after your children, your children also learn what it takes to run a household: they see you doing it and, as they get older, are increasingly called upon to join in and, by and by, to take over tasks. Working together with you in the home teaches your children not only about relevant values, as we have seen, but also about machines, weights, measures, and chemistry, about cleaning techniques and cooking skills, about looking after and organising their physical environment, about taking on responsibility and sharing responsibility with others, and about co-operating and dividing tasks appropriately. And that is good for them, good for you, and good for anybody who is ever going to live with them.

Another strategy for easing your workload is to delegate chores to your children. Your children can learn from an early age to put things back into their place once they have finished with them, to tidy up their room, clear the table, and to get themselves dressed and undressed and to brush their hair. As they grow in maturity and understanding, their responsibilities can become increasingly significant: they can take charge of a family pet or a part of the garden, prepare the occasional meal, look after siblings, and entertain guests. Try and match tasks to your children's abilities and, to some extent, to their interests. Make sure you give your children the freedom to experiment a little; explain to them what needs doing, show them how you do it, then stand back and trust them to find their own way. And remember to delegate without abdicating - ultimately, you are still responsible for what happens and may need to check on progress.[24] If you delegate chores to them, your children learn that you have needs yourself as well as limited energy. They also come to understand family life as a joint project in which they are agents rather than mere consumers. And the knowledge that their contributions to family life are highly valued along with their ever-

---

[24] Julie Lenzer Kirk makes this point in her book *The ParentPreneur Edge: What Parenting teaches about building a successful Business*, Wiley, London (2007).

increasing competence and independence help to build your children's self-confidence and sense of self-worth.[25]

Household chores become much less onerous for both you and your children if they are part of a thought-through routine. If you have spent some time thinking about where, when, and how best to do things, chores can integrate more easily into the rest of your life.[26] After the initial effort to get things going, moreover, chores then get done as a matter of course, without you having to invest thought or nagging every time. So, find a routine that suits both you and your children's schedules and energy levels as well as tastes - some people, for example, can't bear the sight of piles of dirty dishes, others don't mind - then stick to it. And help your children to learn to keep to their routine by making sure they face the consequences of negligence: if they haven't tidied their room, for example, you don't go in to clean it. Obviously, allow for some flexibility to adjust to changing moods and energy levels and, from time to time, change your routine to take into account more significant

---

[25] For more on ways and benefits of delegating chores to your children, see my book *Mothering - a spiritual and practical approach*, St Pauls, London (2007), chapter 5.

[26] For help in considering the where, when, and how of household chores, see Kirk, Louise (2002) *Holy Oil and Elbow Grease*, St Pauls, London as well as Melchior, Anna (2007) *Mothering - a spiritual and practical approach* St Pauls, London (2007), chapter 5.

changes in schedules, needs, interests, and competence. I was so stuck in a rut, for example, that it wasn't until a friend pointed it out to me that I realised that our older children could easily make their sandwiches and pack their lunch boxes themselves. The mornings are a lot more pleasant for me now!

A further strategy to render your workload easier is to make that workload more interesting. If, for example, you cook rather than merely heat up and also have some understanding of nutrition, preparing meals becomes a skilled undertaking which challenges your intelligence and creativity and provides opportunities for growth. There are countless such opportunities proffered by the activities involved in home-making and child-rearing: you can develop your skills and knowledge as nutritionist, chef, ethical consumer, interior decorator, seamstress, childcare expert, counsellor, catechist, tutor, coach, entertainer and more through what you do as a mother!

A fifth strategy of easing your workload involves rethinking that very workload. What, indeed, really needs doing? At the risk of shocking you, I can confess, for instance, that we bathed our babies and small children only once to twice a week; that I often vacuum clean the downstairs only, as the upstairs is still fairly clean; that I only iron every two months or so as, in my view, very few items of clothing require ironing; and that I regularly return clothes left in the dirty laundry bin unwashed to their owners because they do not seem to me to require washing. So perhaps you, too, can cut corners here or there without anybody in your family suffering unduly as a result. Also, could you make your job easier by rearranging your house a little? Could you make space for your children (and visitors?!) to take off and store their shoes near the door so they don't spread dirt from the street throughout the house, thereby making frequent vacuum cleaning less necessary? Might you let your little children have the master bedroom as they could use the greater floor space for their toys, thereby making frequent tidy-ups less necessary? Could you find space for your children to do their homework or practise their instruments in or near the kitchen so you can help them when necessary as well as appreciate their efforts while cooking the evening meal? Are things like recycling bins, lunch boxes, and scissors stored in the most convenient places? You can save yourself a lot of time and hassle by changing some of your assumptions and habits.

Finally, reducing the amount of stuff you have in the house also helps to reduce and therefore to ease your workload. If you have fewer things, you have less to dust, less to wash, and less to tidy away. Sort out toys, clothes, books, gadgets, and trinkets to give to friends or to charity. You could keep a bag or two on the go and pop things in as you notice them. One trick that has helped me in the past is to pretend that we are putting our house on the market. It is amazing how this little pretence can help to focus my mind: all of a sudden, I a) *notice* the piles of papers and toys and whatnots that have lain about untouched for weeks and b) find the time and energy and, what's more, the *will* to deal with them. In a sense, this method of easing your workload is quite similar to the previous one as it also involves taking a second look at what you have taken for granted. Put the things aside for a few weeks to see if anybody misses them. Do consult interested parties, and do keep in mind that you want your home to look like a home still, not like an airport lounge - following a friend's clutter clearance efforts, her daughter complained that her mother had removed "all the beautiful things" from the house. Older children can sort through their own things, perhaps as a condition of acquiring anything new. It helps, of course, if you are in the habit of not buying items unless you have real need or at least good use for them and get your children into the same habit, as well. This restrained approach to consumption saves you money as well as space and work. It also frees you to focus on more important things than things.

Looking after yourself

As a mother, you need to look after yourself on several different levels. Most obviously, there are your physical needs. When your children's needs for good food and rest and exercise keep you busy, it can be easy to forget about your own needs for good food, rest, and exercise. Then there are your social needs. Although children are fascinating and funny and conversations with other parents are enjoyable as well as helpful, you may also want to have a social life that is not dominated by your role as a mother, and that can take extra effort and organisation. Finally, there are, what I would call, your philosophical needs. These are your needs to see meaning in what you do, both from moment to moment and in an overarching sense. It is your ability to find what you do meaningful that, in a very real sense, helps to sustain you as a mother.

When you look after your body, you also look after your head and your heart because you can function better mentally as well as emotionally when you are nourished, rested, and fit. Which mother has not struggled to penetrate the haziness that passes for memory after so many bad nights with the baby? And which mother has not broken down in tears at some point from sheer exhaustion? If you have your children at home full-time, you can ensure that you eat and sleep by eating when they eat and sleeping when they sleep during the day. By eating with your children, you also teach your children that mealtimes are occasions when we take time to appreciate food and each other's company. If you get broken sleep at night, lie down when your baby has a nap. An older sibling can watch a video or play quietly at the same time. As for exercise, you can get plenty by carrying your baby on your back and by walking or cycling to places with your children rather than driving, as well as by doing the housework, gardening, walking the dog, and playing football in the park together with your children. By working with, rather than against, your children's needs for good food, rest, and exercise, you can generally get enough good food, rest, and exercise yourself even as you are busy being a mother.

Socially, as in so many other respects, becoming a mother is generally a turning point. Not only are you preoccupied with getting to know your baby and coming to terms with your responsibilities as a mother, your interests and values also change dramatically. What seemed important before having a baby no longer appears particularly relevant. To some extent, the world-beyond-children along with its values and preoccupations fades into the distance, and new values and preoccupations, different hopes and different worries, take their place. This can be a somewhat disorienting experience as our identities before giving birth were based in that world-beyond-children. It is helpful to be aware of this potential source of insecurity. Meeting up with other new mothers who are experiencing a similar shift in their interests and values and who, I have found, often discuss their concerns and anxieties with great gusto and humour, can help you to forge a new social identity. Parent and toddler groups, the congregations of parents outside schools and nurseries at pick-up time, as well as the families attending the children's liturgy at church are all potential points of contact with like-minded mothers.

In addition, you may find it helpful to maintain a few anchors, as it were, in the world-beyond-children. These could be former colleagues, friends without children, and, not least, your husband. Occasional child-free time with these people will help you to stay in touch with aspects of the world and aspects of yourself that are not child-centred. Common interest groups such as reading circles and voluntary work can also help you to continue to develop and enjoy parts of your identity that do not hinge on being a mother. In time, you will probably want to or need to re-enter the world-beyond-children in order to earn money. You will probably want to do so, however, on changed terms. When the values and interests of women change so that they put the needs of their families first, society ought to recognise that as a good thing and make it possible for mothers - through rewarding part-time work, flexible working hours, and the option of regularly or mainly working from home - to respond both to the needs of their families and to the demands of their jobs without suffering undue strain.

Finally, there is your need for meaning. You may at times struggle with your role as a mother because the complexity, responsibilities, and challenges of the work of a mother are not generally recognised. It can therefore take some hard-headedness on your part to persevere in your work as a mother despite pressures on you suggesting that only paid employment is worthwhile.

As we have seen already throughout this booklet, the work of a mother is profoundly meaningful and valuable. Through the work you do as a mother, you render your children capable of loving themselves and others, you educate your children, both practically and morally, and help your children to develop inner strength and profound purpose and to remain receptive to grace. Through your work in the home, moreover, you promote the health and general well-being of your family, add significant value to everything you purchase, and help to reduce waste and pollution[27]. As a mother, you help to create community and ensure the future of society and of the Church. There is no other work quite as meaningful and valuable in such a variety of ways as the work of a mother.

Mothering, moreover, is challenging and fulfilling work that compares favourably with other occupations. Mothering gives you invaluable time with your children and incomparable autonomy. It provides you with endless opportunities to expand your horizons as you confront a vast variety of challenges. It is a highly complex

---

[27] You help to reduce waste and pollution, for instance, by cooking from scratch, growing your own vegetables, mending clothes, and recycling waste.

undertaking requiring excellent management skills as well as the ability to acquire and apply all manner of knowledge. And it demands extraordinary emotional commitment and extreme perseverance.[28] There are, then, plenty of reasons to see significance in your work as a mother.

Developing your prayer life

Prayer gives you time out, nourishes your soul, exercises your perceptiveness, offers insight and solace, and helps you to maintain trust in God's loving will as well as hope in the face of adversity. With regular practice, prayer can also help you to develop attitudes which support your work as a mother, namely gratitude, a spirit of service, contemplativeness, and trust. Prayer, moreover, provides a fruitful contrast to the seemingly ceaseless busyness of mothering. By interrupting the flow of your activities to pray, you give yourself the chance to recharge on all fronts.

Short prayers throughout the day, perhaps said together with your children, can help to remind you of God's unwavering presence and love. Through aspirations prayed in the midst of your work, you can entrust this concern to God, share with Him that resolution, and thank Him for every grace you receive as you go about your work. Gratitude is an especially helpful attitude to

---

[28] This paragraph is adapted from Melchior, Anna (2007), *Mothering - a spiritual and practical approach*, St Pauls, London, p 155.

develop as a mother. It is so easy to look around and only notice our work and our worries and fail to see our many blessings. So try to make a habit of noticing and thanking God for everything that is good in your children's lives, in your life, and in your lives together. This practice will help you to approach both your children and your work as a mother more positively, and that will make your relationship with your children and your work as a mother much easier.

Prayer can also help you to adopt a spirit of service which helps you to understand the many unglamorous tasks that are a necessary part of being a mother as sanctifying labour. By doing whatever you do to the best of your ability for the love of others and for the love of God, you can imbue the humblest chore with transcendental meaning, you can convert work into prayer, as St Josemaria Escriva put it. What is good advice for monks is also good advice for mothers: 'do cheerfully and faithfully what duty asks of you and that will teach you what you need to know to come to God.'[29] By cleaning the toilet, mopping up sick, or combing out nits from your children's hair in such a spirit of service, you develop the virtues of patience and fortitude which will stand you in good stead when you come up against

---

[29] Fr Ronald Rolheiser, 'The Secret of a monk's cell', *The Catholic Herald*, 16th May 2008.

greater challenges. And when, like St Thérèse of Lisieux, you find yourself welcoming every such chance to practise abdication of self-will, you know that you are well on your way to sainthood!

By regularly taking time away from the demands of your children and the household to pray in front of the Blessed Sacrament, you can regain, if necessary, or else strengthen that inner calm on which not only you but your entire family rely. Leave your worries on the altar and let your body become a tabernacle and so allow your centre to become calm and peaceful and persevering and loving and giving and humble and holy like the host inside it. Prayer in front of the Blessed Sacrament can be an emptying of self, a handing over, as it were, of all your current concerns and preoccupations. And after you have thus emptied yourself, you can receive God's strength and graces. This form of prayer is very like meditation and similarly restorative. It also renders you receptive to the fruits of the Holy Spirit which are love, joy, peace, patience, kindness, goodness, trustfulness, gentleness, and self-control (*Ga* 5:22-23) - all very useful qualities to have if you are a mother! Regularly tapping into God's calm presence for twenty minutes or so, moreover, gradually enables you to tap into that sea of calm even in the middle of those hectic moments.

Prayer also helps with the big issues. Prayer allows us to step back from the fight and to shift it onto a higher plane, closer to God's saving grace. When I am in regular conflict with one of our children and cannot see a way out, for example, I force myself to stop and pray about the situation and to pray for that child in particular. By and by, prayer and patience opens me to grace and to the changes for good worked by grace. Prayer offers hope when we are at our wits' end, when love and reason and good example and parenting skills seem to no avail. Much can be accomplished through prayer. St Augustine led a dissolute life but, in time, his mother St Monica converted him through prayer and patience. Especially as your children grow in independence, keeping them in your prayer is a way of keeping them close to God.

Prayer, finally, helps you to surrender your will to God. Often, we do not understand what is happening in our lives and we do not understand why bad things happen. Unemployment, marital difficulties, severe illness, and the death of loved ones can throw us off balance. At times like this, faith and trust in God's loving will, developed through prayer, help us to feel held by God even in the midst of inner and outer turmoil. Two years ago, I confronted the fact that I had breast cancer. For the first time in my life, I experienced the fear of death physically and immediately. The fear effectively paralysed me spiritually and I found prayer a real challenge. Eventually, I met that challenge and I am grateful, for I would not want to go through such a painful period without recourse to prayer. Prayer helps us to acknowledge that we do not, after all - and after all our plans and struggles - know what is best. Prayer helps us to trust that God knows what is best and to trust that, in time, we will understand. Trusting in God's loving will and looking for God's hand at work in our difficulties enables us to use well what we have been given, both the good and the bad. Our Lady accompanied our Lord. True greatness can grow out of suffering. Christ showed us how in his Way of the Cross.

And the cross, of course, is the ultimate sign of hope. While the cross is an instrument of torture and was and is the instrument of our Lord's death, it is also the instrument of our redemption. Without the cross, we would be without supernatural hope. But Christ died on the cross and he rose again, atoning for our sin and overcoming death, once and for all. We do not have to die but can live in Christ, here and now, and in the hereafter. Supernatural hope can suffuse our every moment; it shifts into perspective the trials we endure and helps us to look beyond these towards the glory awaiting us. Supernatural hope helps us to battle on because we know that the goal is worth our every effort.

Mothers and others

Mothers necessarily work in a particular context. That context is made up of their relationship to their child's father, other family relationships, friendships, neighbourhood and church communities, working environments, society at large with its policies and economic structures affecting families as well as its media portrayals of the work of mothers, and the Church and its teachings on the family and family-support services. The context in which mothers work and with which they interact can determine whether or not mothers feel valued and fulfilled in their work. It can also make all the difference between positive and negative outcomes for children. While advising mothers is good and useful, then, it is not in itself sufficient. To improve the lot of mothers and therefore the lot of families generally and that of children in particular also requires ensuring that the context in which mothers work supports them in their mothering.

Mothers and fathers

I once spent six weeks looking after our four children and running the household on my own while also finishing a book because my husband was working in the USA for that period. Now, I take some pride in my practical efficiency and relative emotional self-sufficiency, so I did not expect to find those six weeks a struggle, but a struggle they were! I could never ever switch off, not once; if anything needed responding to, it was up to me to respond. After six weeks I'd had enough, and I did not even have to face the financial worries that confront many single mothers. My own mother was a single mother of three and worked as a teacher and lived in a foreign country, at that. She managed, but it was difficult and lonely and stressful for her.

The role of a husband in supporting his wife in her mothering is absolutely vital. His emotional, practical, social, and financial support allows the new mother the time and the space to be there for their baby, to bond with their baby and to grow into her identity as a mother. Over the years, he is there to help set the tone of family life and to share in both the delights and the difficulties of mothering - if not always immediately, then through conversations, reflections, jokes, and a mutual exploring of possibilities at the end of the day - as well as to take over completely from time to time when his wife is away or wants a break. As a father, he nurtures and guides his children. By treating his children with love and respect, he helps them to develop self-esteem. He provides a male role model for his sons and helps them to enjoy as well as to control their developing physical strength. And as one half of a couple, he teaches his children together with his wife about commitment and respect, about compromise and conflict-resolution, about forgiveness and reconciliation. The support of the husband and the involvement of the father help to make mothering manageable for the mother, significantly improve the life chances of their children, and benefit the husband and father himself in countless ways as he, too, discovers the joys of self-giving.

Research shows that married couples live longer lives, enjoy better physical and mental health, and are less likely to suffer domestic violence than people who are cohabiting, divorced, or single. Research also shows invariably that the children of married couples enjoy better mental and physical health, do better academically, and are less likely to run away from home than the children of single, divorced, or cohabiting parents. Cohabiting couples across income brackets are at least twice as likely to split up than married couples.[30] It is marriage, therefore, rather than any alternative arrangement, that consistently promotes the well-being of couples and children. Given this irrefutable evidence, it makes good sense to help couples to get married and to stay married. Acknowledging the importance of fathers as

---

[30] Harry Benson, 'The conflation of marriage and cohabitation in government statistics - a denial of difference rendered untenable by analysis of outcomes', Bristol Community Family Trust, September 2006.

well as marriage preparation courses, marriage counselling, and tax incentives for married couples[31] are some means of doing so. Any costs involved are more than compensated for by the savings to the tax payer brought about by increased family stability.[32]

Mothers and the community

Mothers are an essential part of any community. Through their daily interaction with each other and with other members of the community, mothers ensure that the community exists not merely on the map but in word and deed - in sharing concerns and childcare with other parents, helping neighbours out, supporting local businesses, raising funds for improvements to the local school, organising and helping at events at the local church, and so forth. Because they are focused on their children's well-being, mothers are also usually the first to detect and address problems in the community that are detrimental to their children's development, such as bullying behaviour and speeding motorists. Mothers are the ones who create safe places to be, both in their homes

---

[31] Tax incentives could be key as it is often financial concerns that prevent a couple from committing to marriage, according to a report by the think tank Civitas, *The Press Association*, 19th May 2008.

[32] The cost to society of divorce as well as of diet-related poor health, behavioural difficulties, anti-social behaviour, delinquency, and substance abuse among the young is enormous.

and in their communities.[33] Most importantly, by having children and by raising their children well - by recreating life and love - mothers help to create a better future for their community and for society at large.

But to what extent do communities support mothers in their mothering? Mothers can and do help themselves by creating their own networks of child-friendly and supportive friends and neighbours, baby-sitting circles, and parent-and-toddler groups. There are other factors which mothers cannot control directly, however, which significantly affect the extent to which a community supports the work of mothers. Do local surgeries offer antenatal as well as post-natal mothering classes and provide specially trained counsellors for pregnant women in particularly difficult circumstances as well as teams of mothers' mentors to support mothers in the months following the birth of a baby? Are there affordable houses available, houses with gardens large enough for families but not so expensive as to require two incomes to finance? Are there communal areas in the neighbourhood where parents can meet and casually share childcare? Do roads have a 20 mph speed limit in residential areas so that children can cross safely? Are there parks and

---

[33] 'We women have always been the ones to construct and piece together sanctuary and refuge for all our people - our neighbourhoods, our family.' June Jordan cited in Exley, Helen (1998), *Thoughts on Being a Mother*, Exley Publications, New York.

playgrounds to explore? Is there a choice of playgroups that offer pre-school children a few hours away from home and mothers time-off? Are families with small children made welcome at the local church and integrated into services? Are discreetly breastfeeding mothers welcome in local restaurants and cafés? Do these restaurants and cafés offer nutritious and affordable meals for children? Is there a local library with a good selection of children's books? Are local schools well resourced? Are there church-run youth groups? Are there sports clubs? Are there opportunities for youngsters to do voluntary work and contribute to their communities? The childcare expert Steve Biddulph emphasises the crucial importance of community in supporting mothering: 'When families are woven in with friends and neighbours, and when people of all generations have access to each other, then we won't need psychologists or departments of social welfare. We'll take care of ourselves.'[34]

Mothers and society

While I receive leaflets from our city council urging me to hand over our children to full-time childcare facilities as that would supposedly benefit both them and me in numerous ways, that same council also advises me to

[34] Biddulph, Steve (1998), *The Secret of Happy Children*, Thorsons, London, 138.

give our children love and affection, time and attention, to set clear limits, to teach them right from wrong, make time for play, get involved with their education, get them used to healthy food, to read with them and to get outdoors and moving with them, as well as to look after myself. Does nobody in the council realise that following all this excellent parenting advice TAKES A LOT OF TIME, TIME NOT SPENT AWAY AT WORK? It seems to me that, with respect to mothering, there is a profound case of schizophrenia imbedded in government, a case of being out of touch with reality, and the contradictory messages from the local council are only one of its many manifestations.

In the current climate, it takes guts and determination to decide to focus on mothering. Not only do government propaganda and policies aim to replace mothers with institutional childcare and employers rarely accommodate the wish to mother, but our wider society with its preoccupation with money and measurable achievement as well as its disdain for commitment also utterly fails to recognise the crucially important contribution to society made by mothers who raise well-balanced children. The journalist Tara Winter Wilson notes that 'mothers who choose to stay at home with their children are routinely dismissed [...] and sneered at as "non-people".'[35] This is

---

[35] *The Daily Telegraph*, 1st March 2007.

how a mother of two describes the cultural landscape in which mothers find themselves:

> The 'real world' is the male-dominated world of work. Women can enter that world but must leave all their dreary concerns about children, home-making etc behind when they do so. The world they then enter is colourful, vibrant and rewarding. Motherhood in this context is pushed to the grey, colourless periphery of life. Mothers are ciphers or ghosts who live some sort of half-life - dispossessed and cut off from the real world.[36]

The challenge we face, therefore, is not only that of restructuring the tax system and the work place to accommodate better the needs of families, but also that of effecting a cultural change, a change in values. Kate Figes, journalist, author, and mother, writes of the need for a 'wider cultural change which acknowledges the importance of motherhood and accepts mothers' very special needs'.[37] Cardinal Ratzinger, now Pope Benedict XVI, formulated the challenge as follows:

> The harmonisation of the organisation of work and laws governing work with the demands stemming from the mission of women within the family is a challenge.

---

[36] Alison Hawdale, in an e-mail to the author, December 2007.

[37] Figes, Kate (1998), *Life after Birth*, Penguin Books, London.

The question is not only legal, economic, and organisational; it is above all a question of mentality, culture, and respect. Indeed, a just valuing of the work of women within the family is required. In this way, women who freely desire will be able to devote the totality of their time to the work of the household without being stigmatised by society and penalised financially, while those who wish also to engage in other work may be able to do so with an appropriate work-schedule, and not have to choose between relinquishing their family life or enduring continual stress, with negative consequences for one's own equilibrium and the harmony of the family.[38]

Mothers need 'a society and an economy that recognise, respect, and back their work in the home.'[39]

I have already mentioned ways of meeting the policy aspect of this challenge in other sections of this booklet. In addition to these, income splitting, in which the combined income of a couple is split into two halves for tax rate purposes would help couples in which one of the partners earns nothing or very little because they look after the children. A child tax allowance, moreover, would

---

[38] Congregation for the Doctrine of the Faith, *On the Collaboration of Men and Women in the Church and in the World* (2004), p 13.

[39] Melchior, Anna (2007), *Mothering - a spiritual and practical approach*, St Pauls, London, p 160.

give parents real choice as it would allow them to decide themselves whether to use professional childcare, pay friends or family members to help look after their children, or look after their children themselves. Income splitting and a child tax allowance, incidentally, require significantly less administration than a system of subsidised childcare. Paying mothers who stay at home to look after their pre-school children a modest income would boost morale among mothers as it would imply recognition of the value of the work they are doing, as well as facilitate that work as it would alleviate some of the financial pressures on families. Subsidising fresh fruit and vegetables or else providing lower- and middle-income families with fruit and vegetable vouchers would help mothers to feed the plagues of locusts (their children). Mothers of disabled children or children with special needs should receive the additional support they require as a matter of course.[40] Recognising in law and in practice the pre-eminent authority of parents over their children should be another matter of course. Besides the right in law to flexible working hours and rewarding part-time jobs as well as the option of working for home, many mothers would also benefit from back-to-work guidance to help to ease them back into paid employment

---

[40] It strikes me as unreasonable that the state offers far greater assistance to a disabled child's carer if that carer is a foster parent than if that carer is the birth parent.

after years of mainly mothering as well as from support specifically geared to help mothers to set up and run their own businesses, as many mothers welcome the relative flexibility that running a business can afford. Careers counselling in schools could make school leavers aware of the problems confronting parents in the workplace and help them to consider appropriate solutions for themselves long before they have children.

There are several ways to take up the cultural aspect of the challenge. One way is to get more people - husbands as well as friends and neighbours, aunts and uncles, your own and others' older children - involved in mothering so that they understand better both the demands and the rewards of the job (and so as to give you a break, as well!). Otherwise, with children tucked away in institutions for most of the day, mothering will increasingly become an unappreciated lost art.[41] Another way is to speak up for the work of mothering - on whatever scale you can. A friend recently rebuked me (mildly) after I had replied to the question 'what do you do'? at one of her smart parties with 'I am a housewife'. Given the scientists, academics, artists, and actors attending that party, it was a subversive reply. In

---

[41] Many career politicians probably promote institutional childcare not least because they themselves have relegated the care of their children to others and therefore know little about the work involved.

Germany, the Catholic psychotherapist and author Christa Meves has been campaigning for some forty years through publications[42] and talks for the popular and political recognition of the work of mothering, for, what she aptly terms, *a renaissance of mothers*. I wrote my book, *Mothering*, as a contribution to that urgently needed cultural change which will see mothers both valued and supported in their work. The mother of two cited above commented that the account of mothering I give in the book turns the cultural landscape of mothers described earlier on its head; I end this booklet with her inspirational words:

> Mothering is the glowing, vibrant heart of society. It is the heart of the family, which is at the heart of the community, which is at the heart of society. Good mothering underpins and provides a foundation for all other endeavours in the world. Reading your book made me feel that what I'm doing is real, valuable and just as interesting and exciting (if not more so) than many aspects of the world of paid work. That I haven't opted out of life, but am doing something essential and rewarding.[43]

---

[42] Among her many insightful as well as helpful publications, Christa Meves' books *Geheimnis Gehirn* and *Erziehen Lernen*, both published by Resch Verlag, Germany, are particularly noteworthy.

[43] Alison Hawdale, op. cit.

The Role of A Christian Father

In a time when the very idea of the Christian family is being lost, the role of the father has been devalued to the point of seeming optional. This booklet looks at this most delicate but formative of relationships exploring it historically, and in the scriptures but also giving present-day examples and practical advice on how a father can lead his children and his family to fulfilment, happiness and faith.

Keith Chappell studied at the Maryvale Institute in Birmingham and Oxford University, teaches theology and works as a family mediator. He lives in Berkshire with his wife Maeve and their two children.

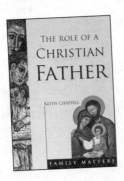

ISBN: 978 1 86082 514 9

CTS Code: PA 11

The Role of Christian Grandparents

We live in a time of constant change, when the latest fashions and technology dominate popular culture, and society seems to be moving further away from God. Yet the role of grandparents – in a society where life expectancy is growing, and often both parents work – is becoming stronger. This booklet explores how grandparents can be present in the lives of their grandchildren to pass on the wisdom they have gained and the faith they have received.

The Family Matters series encourages a journey in faith, creativity and initiative, offering practical proposals for families to flourish in the love of God.

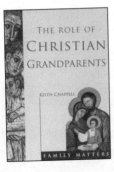

Keith Chappell studied at the Maryvale Institute in Birmingham and Oxford University, teaches theology and works as a family mediator. He lives in Berkshire with his wife Maeve and their two children.

ISBN: 978 1 86082 635 1

CTS Code: PA 15

Prayer Book for Spouses

These prayers and meditations offer couples a ready, thorough and reliable support to the daily challenges and joys of married life. Drawing on Scripture, Catholic teaching and spirituality, and the Marriage Rite itself, this prayer book encourages the loving and spiritual dimension essential to the life of Christian spouses. Their care of each other, their openness to life, love for their children and wider family, as well their willing co-operation with the will of a loving Father and their courage to face life's difficulties with faith - all this forms the tapestry of which Christian marriages, rooted in a love of God and neighbour, are made.

Contributors and advisers: Adrian Treloar, Amette Ley, Bernard Toutounji, David Baldwin, Edmund Adamus, Fiorella Nash, Jennifer Moorcroft, Joanna Bogle, Josephine Robinson, Nick and Martina Donnelly, Rev Tim Finigan, Tim Tindal-Robertson.

ISBN: 978 1 86082 617 7

CTS Code: D 714

Sexuality and Love

On this issue more than any other the Church seems out of step with the modern world, yet she refuses to compromise. Fr Gasparino tackles the most difficult problems showing that the Church does not want to limit people's lives. On the contrary, she follows Christ in teaching how to live a generous honest love that is free and pure.

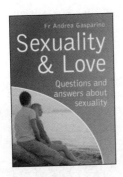

ISBN: 978 1 86082 296 4

CTS Code: PA 1

The Special Gift of Women

In a time when the very idea of the Christian family is being lost, the role of the father has been devalued to the point of seeming optional. This booklet looks at this most delicate but formative of relationships exploring it historically, and in the scriptures but also giving present-day examples and practical advice on how a father can lead his children and his family to fulfilment, happiness and faith.

Keith Chappell studied at the Maryvale Institute in Birmingham and Oxford University, teaches theology and works as a family mediator. He lives in Berkshire with his wife Maeve and their two children.

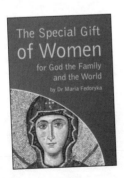

ISBN: 978 1 86082 678 8

CTS Code: Do 830